PIANO • VOCAL • GUITAR

Smoky Mountain
Gospel Favorites

A COLLECTION OF 37 TIMELESS GOSPEL HYMNS

D1540696

ISBN 0-7935-6940-0

HAL•LEONARD®
CORPORATION

7777 W. BLUEMOUND RD. P.O. BOX 13819 MILWAUKEE, WI 53213

Visit Hal Leonard on the internet at http://www.halleonard.com

PIANO • VOCAL • GUITAR

Smoky Mountain Gospel Favorites

A COLLECTION OF 37 TIMELESS GOSPEL HYMNS

AMAZING GRACE

Words by JOHN NEWTON
Traditional American Melody

taught my heart to fear and grace my fears re-lieved.
prom-ised good to me, His word my hope se-cures.

How pre-cious did that grace ap-pear the
He will my shield and por-tion be as

hour I first be-lieved. 2. Through
long as life en-dures.

Verse 3
And when this flesh and heart shall fail
and mortal life shall cease.
I shall possess within the veil
a life of joy and peace.

When we've been there ten thousand years,
bright shining as the sun.

We've no less days to sing God's praise
than when we first begun.

ARE YOU WASHED IN THE BLOOD

Traditional

1. Have you been to Je - sus for the cleans - ing pow'r? Are you
2.-4. *(See additional lyrics)*

washed in the blood of the Lamb? Are you full - y trust - ing in His

grace this hour? Are you washed in the blood of the Lamb? Are you

Refrain

Additional Lyrics

2. Are you walking daily by the Savior's side?
    Are you washed in the blood of the Lamb?
    Do you rest each moment in the Crucified?
    Are you washed in the blood of the Lamb?
    REFRAIN

3. When the Bridegroom cometh will your robes be white?
    Are you washed in the blood of the Lamb?
    Will your soul be ready for the mansions bright,
    And be washed in the blood of the Lamb?
    REFRAIN

4. Lay aside the garments that are stained with sin,
    And be washed in the blood of the Lamb;
    There's a fountain flowing for the soul unclean,
    O be washed in the blood of the Lamb!
    REFRAIN

AT CALVARY

Traditional

1. Years I spent in van - i - ty and pride,
2.-4. *(See additional lyrics)*

Car - ing not my Lord was cru - ci - fied, Know - ing not it was for me He died On Cal - va - ry.

Additional Lyrics

2. By God's Word at last my sin I learned;
    Then I trembled at the law I'd spurned,
    Till my guilty soul imploring turned To Calvary.
    REFRAIN

3. Now I've giv'n to Jesus ev'rything,
    Now I gladly own Him as my King,
    Now my raptured soul can only sing Of Calvary.
    REFRAIN

4. Oh, the love that drew salvation's plan!
    Oh, the grace that bro't it down to man!
    Oh, the mighty gulf that God did span At Calvary.
    REFRAIN

AT THE CROSS

Text by ISAAC WATTS
Music by RALPH E. HUDSON

BEULAH LAND

Traditional

1. I've reached the land of
2.,3. *(See additional lyrics)*

love di-vine And all its rich - es free - ly mine; Here shines un-dimmed one

bliss - ful day, For all my night has passed a-way. O Beu - lah Land, sweet

Additional Lyrics

2. My Savior comes and walks with me,
   And sweet communion here have we;
   He gently leads me by His hand,
   For this is heaven's borderland.
   REFRAIN

3. The zephyrs seem to float to me,
   Sweet sounds of heaven's melody,
   As angels with the white-robed throng
   Join in the sweet Redemption song.
   REFRAIN

BLESSED ASSURANCE

Lyrics by FANNY CROSBY and VAN ALSTYNE
Music by PHOEBE P. KNAPP

With movement

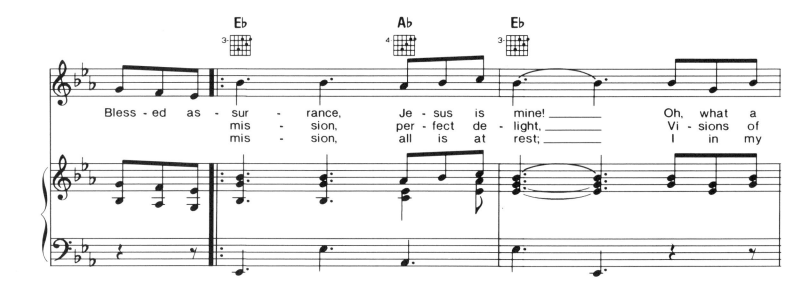

Bless - ed as - sur - rance, Je - sus is mine! _____ Oh, what a
mis - sion, per - fect de - light, _____ Vi - sions of
mis - sion, all is at rest; _____ I in my

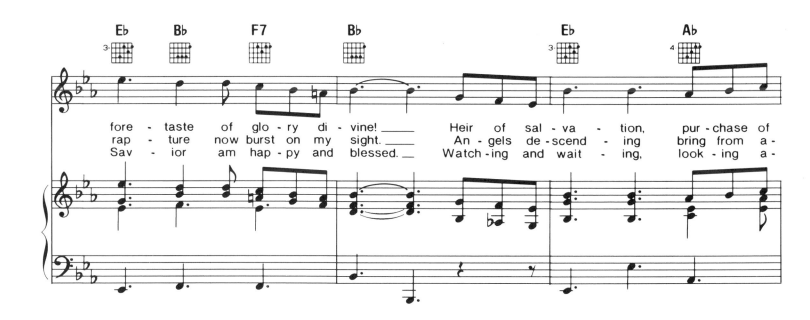

fore - taste of glo - ry di - vine! _____ Heir of sal - va - tion, pur - chase of
rap - ture now burst on my sight. _____ An - gels de - scend - ing bring from a -
Sav - ior am hap - py and blessed. _ Watch - ing and wait - ing, look - ing a -

CHURCH IN THE WILDWOOD

Traditional

2. O come to the church in the wildwood,
   To the trees where the wild flowers bloom;
   Where the parting hymn will be changed,
   We will weep by the side of the tomb.

3. From the church in the valley by the wildwood,
   When day fades away into night,
   I would fain from this spot of my childhood,
   Wing my way to the mansions of light.

HAVE THINE OWN WAY, LORD

Words by ADELAIDE POLLARD
Music by GEORGE STEBBINS

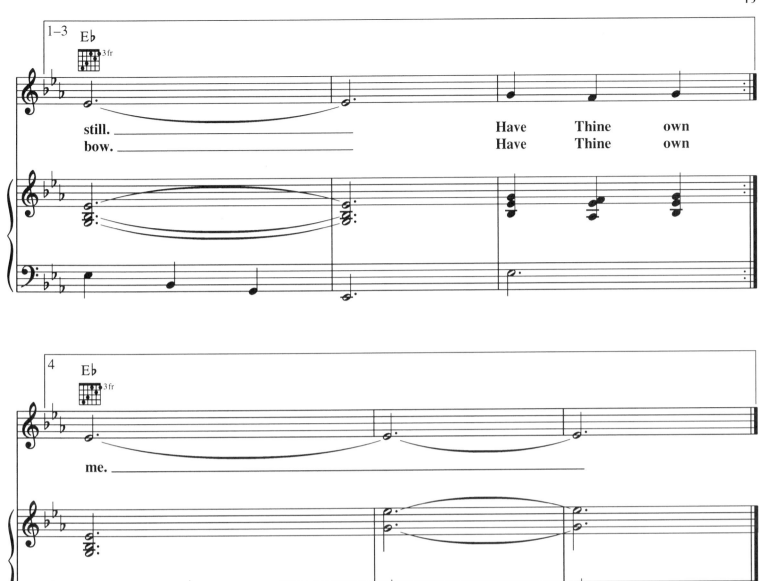

Additional Lyrics

3. Have Thine own way, Lord!
   Have Thine own way!
   Wounded and weary, Help me, I pray!
   Power, all power
   Surely is Thine!
   Touch me and heal me, Savior divine.

4. Have Thine own way, Lord!
   Have Thine own way!
   Hold o'er my being Absolute sway!
   Fill with Thy Spirit
   Till all shall see
   Christ only, always, Living in me.

I AM BOUND
FOR THE PROMISED LAND

Traditional

Lyrics:

1. On __ Jor - dan's _ storm - y
2., 3. *(See additional lyrics)*

banks I __ stand, __ And cast a __ wish - ful eye, To __ Ca - naan's _ fair and hap - py land, Where __ my pos - ses - sions lie. I am bound for the prom - ised

land, prom-ised land, _ I am bound for the prom - ised land; Oh, _ who will _ come and

go with me? I am bound for the prom - ised land. O'er _ land.

Descant *(sing during refrains only)*

Oh, yes, I'm go-ing to __ Glo-ry Land; Oh, yes, I'll sing _ in that an - gel band.

"Tell me the old, old sto - ry" I'm bound for heav'ns _ glo - ry land.

Additional Lyrics

2. O'er all those wide extended plains
   Shines one eternal day,
   There God the Son forever reigns
   And scatters night away.
   REFRAIN

3. When shall I reach that happy place,
   And be forever blest?
   When shall I see the Father's face,
   And in His bosom rest?
   REFRAIN

I LOVE TO TELL THE STORY

By K. HANKEY and W.G. FISCHER

24

I'VE GOT PEACE LIKE A RIVER

Traditional

IN THE GARDEN

Words and Music by
C. AUSTIN MILES

I come to the gar-den a-lone, _____ while the
speaks, and the sound of His voice _____ is so

dew is still on the ros - es; and the voice I
sweet the still birds hush their sing - ing; and the mel - o -

hear, fall-ing on my ear, the Son of God dis-
-dy that He gave to me with-in of my heart is

IN THE SWEET BY AND BY

Traditional

JUST AS I AM

Words by CARLOTTE ELLIOTT
Music by WM. BRADBURY

Slowly, with movement

ROCK OF AGES

Text by AUGUSTUS M. TOPLADY
Music by THOMAS HASTINGS

3. While I draw this fleeting breath,
   When my eyes shall close in death,
   When I rise to worlds unknown,
   And behold Thee on Thy throne,
   Rock Of Ages cleft for me,
   Let me hide myself in Thee.

JUST OVER IN THE GLORYLAND

Traditional

Additional Lyrics

2. I am on my way to those mansions fair,
    Just over in the glory land;
    There to sing God's praise and His glory share,
    Just over in the glory land.
    REFRAIN

3. What a joyful tho't that my Lord I'll see,
    Just over in the glory land;
    And with kindred saved there forever be,
    Just over in the glory land.
    REFRAIN

4. With the blood-washed throng I will shout and sing,
    Just over in the glory land;
    Glad hosannas to Christ, the Lord and King,
    Just over in the glory land.
    REFRAIN

THE LILY OF THE VALLEY

Traditional

Additional Lyrics

2. He all my grief has taken, and all my sorrows borne;
   In temptation He's my strong and mighty tow'r;
   I have all for Him forsaken, and all my idols torn
   From my heart and now He keeps me by His pow'r.
   Though all the world forsake me, and Satan tempt me sore,
   Through Jesus I shall safely reach the goal:
   REFRAIN

3. He will never, never leave me, nor yet forsake me here,
   While I live by faith and do His blessed will;
   A wall of fire about me, I've nothing now to fear,
   With His manna He my hungry soul shall fill.
   Then sweeping up to glory to see His blessed face,
   Where rivers of delight shall ever roll:
   REFRAIN

NEAR THE CROSS

Traditional

Additional Lyrics

2. Near the cross, a trembling soul,
   Love and mercy found me;
   There the bright and Morning Star
   Sheds its beams around me.
   REFRAIN

3. Near the cross! O Lamb of God,
   Bring its scenes before me;
   Help me walk from day to day,
   With its shadows o'er me.
   REFRAIN

4. Near the cross I'll watch and wait,
   Hoping, trusting ever,
   Till I reach the golden strand,
   Just beyond the river.
   REFRAIN

NOTHING BUT THE BLOOD

Words and Music by
ROBERT LOWRY

Additional Lyrics

2. For my pardon this I see
    Nothing but the blood of Jesus;
    For my cleansing this my plea
    Nothing but the blood of Jesus.
    REFRAIN

3. Nothing can for sin atone
    Nothing but the blood of Jesus;
    Naught of good that I have done
    Nothing but the blood of Jesus.
    REFRAIN

THE OLD RUGGED CROSS

By REV. GEORGE BENNARD

PASS ME NOT, O GENTLE SAVIOR

Traditional

Additional Lyrics

2. Let me at your throne of mercy find a sweet relief;
   Kneeling there in deep contrition, help my unbelief.
   REFRAIN

3. Trusting only in your merit, would I seek your face;
   Heal my wounded, broken spirit, save me by your grace.
   REFRAIN

4. Be the Spring of all my comfort, more than life to me;
   Not just here on earth beside me, but eternally.
   REFRAIN

POWER IN THE BLOOD

Traditional

Additional Lyrics

2. Would you be free from your passion and pride?
There's pow'r in the blood, pow'r in the blood;
Come for a cleansing to Calvary's tide;
There's wonderful pow'r in the blood.
REFRAIN

3. Would you be whiter, much whiter than snow?
There's pow'r in the blood, pow'r in the blood;
Sin stains are lost in its lifegiving flow;
There's wonderful pow'r in the blood.
REFRAIN

4. Would you do service for Jesus your King?
There's pow'r in the blood, pow'r in the blood;
Would you live daily His praises to sing?
There's wonderful pow'r in the blood.
REFRAIN

SEND THE LIGHT

Traditional

Additional Lyrics

2. We have heard the Macedonian call today:
   Send the light! Send the light!
   And a golden off'ring at the cross we lay:
   Send the light! Send the light!
   REFRAIN

3. Let us pray that grace may ev'rywhere abound:
   Send the light! Send the light!
   And a Christ-like spirit ev'rywhere be found:
   Send the light! Send the light!
   REFRAIN

4. Let us not grow weary in the work of love:
   Send the light! Send the light!
   Let us gather jewels for a crown above:
   Send the light! Send the light!
   REFRAIN

SHALL WE GATHER AT THE RIVER

Words and Music by
ROBERT LOWRY

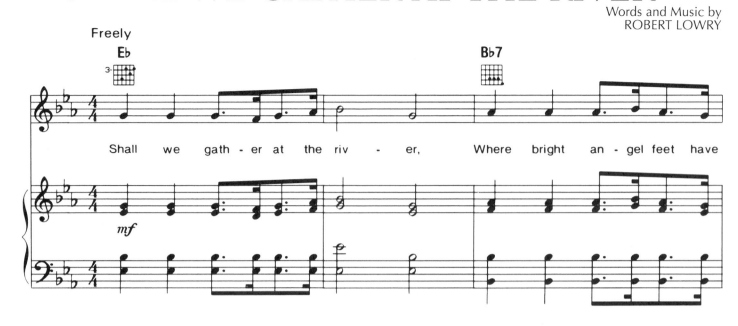

Shall we gath-er at the riv - er, Where bright an-gel feet have

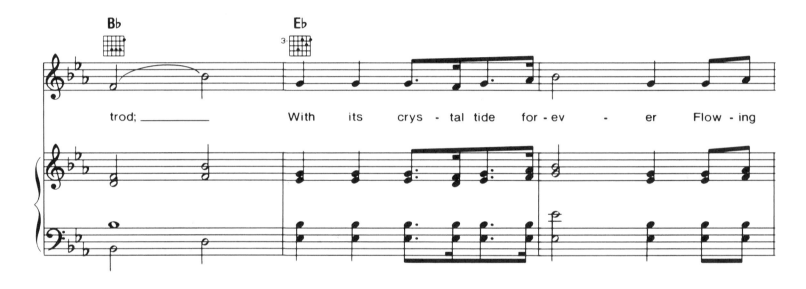

trod; _____ With its crys-tal tide for-ev - er Flow-ing

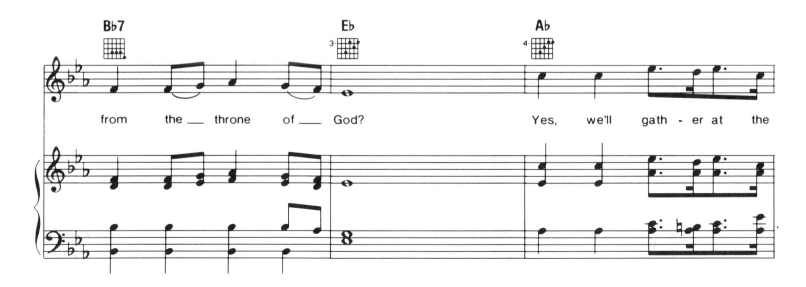

from the __ throne of __ God? Yes, we'll gath - er at the

river, The beau - ti - ful, the beau - ti - ful ___ riv - er,

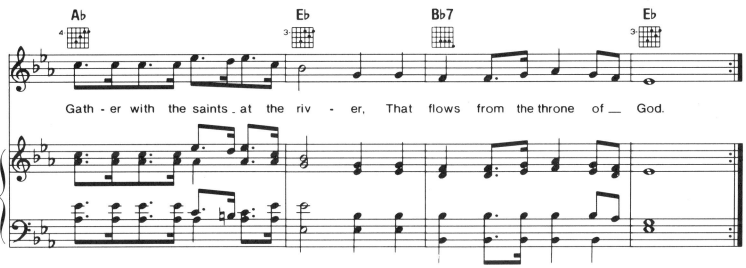

Gath - er with the saints _ at the riv - er, That flows from the throne of __ God.

2. On the margin of the river,
   Washing up its silver spray,
   We shall walk and worship ever
   All the happy, golden day.

3. On the bosom of the river,
   Where the Saviour King we own,
   We shall meet and sorrow never
   'Neath the glory of the throne.

4. Ere we reach the shining river,
   Lay we ev'ry burden down:
   Grace our spirits will deliver,
   And provide a robe and crown.

5. Soon we'll reach the shining river,
   Soon our pilgrimage will cease;
   Soon our happy hearts will quiver
   With the melody of peace.

SINCE JESUS CAME INTO MY HEART

Words by R.H. McDANIEL
Music by CHARLES H. GABRIEL

Additional Lyrics

3. There's a light in the valley of death now for me,
   Since Jesus came into my heart!
   And the gates of the city beyond I can see,
   Since Jesus came into my heart!
   REFRAIN

4. I shall go there to dwell in that city, I know,
   Since Jesus came into my heart!
   And I'm happy, so happy, as onward I go,
   Since Jesus came into my heart!
   REFRAIN

SOFTLY AND TENDERLY

By WILL L. THOMPSON

Moderately Slow

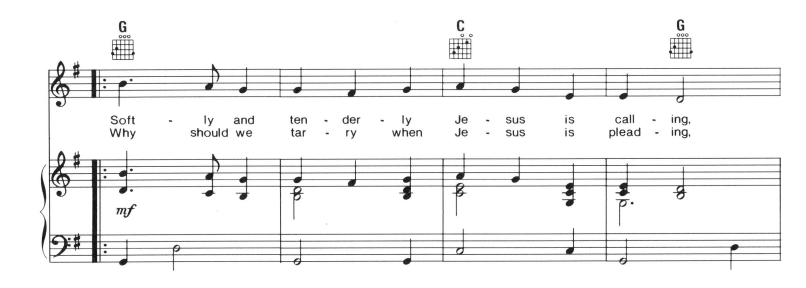

Soft - ly and ten - der - ly Je - sus is call - ing,
Why should we tar - ry when Je - sus is plead - ing,

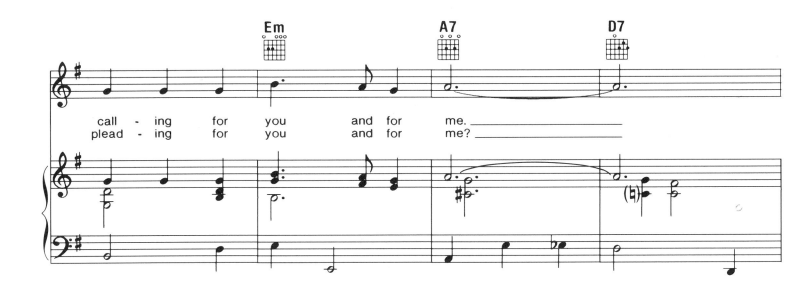

call - ing for you and for me. _____
plead - ing for you and for me? _____

STANDING ON THE PROMISES

Traditional

Additional Lyrics

2. Standing on the promises that cannot fail,
   When the howling storms of doubt and fear assail,
   By the living word of God I shall prevail,
   Standing on the promises of God.
   REFRAIN

3. Standing on the promises of Christ the Lord,
   Bound to Him eternally by love's strong cord,
   Overcoming daily with the Spirit's sword,
   Standing on the promises of God.
   REFRAIN

4. Standing on the promises I cannot fall,
   Listening ev'ry moment to the Spirit's call,
   Resting in my Savior as my all in all,
   Standing on the promises of God.
   REFRAIN

SWEET HOUR OF PRAYER

By W.W. WALFORD and W.B. BRADBURY

Moderately

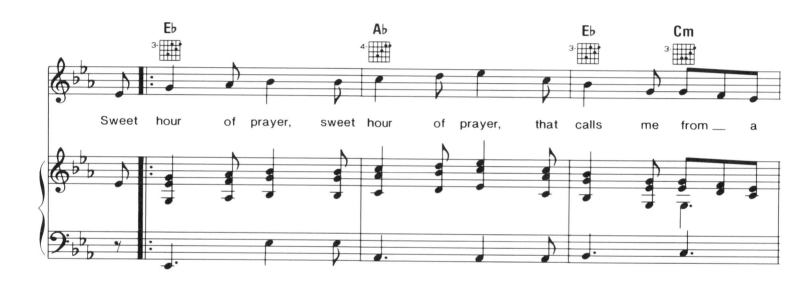

Sweet hour of prayer, sweet hour of prayer, that calls me from __ a

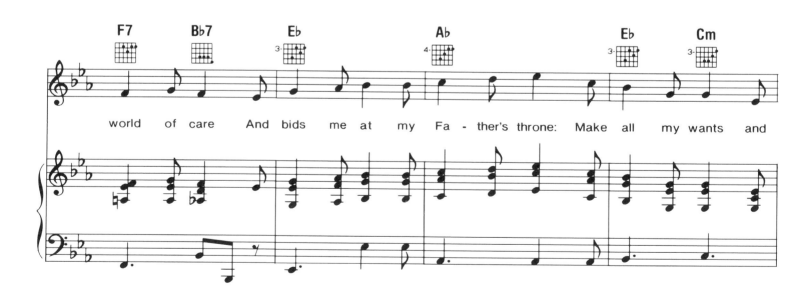

world of care And bids me at my Fa - ther's throne: Make all my wants and

2. (Sweet) hour of prayer,
   Sweet hour of prayer,
   thy wings shall my petition bear
   To Him whose truth and faithfulness
   engage the waiting soul to bless.
   And since He bids me seek His face,
   believe His word, and trust His grace,
   I'll cast on Him my ev'ry care
   and wait for thee, sweet hour of prayer.

3. (Sweet) hour of prayer,
   sweet hour of prayer,
   may I thy consolation share
   Till from Mount Pisgah's lofty height
   I view my home and take my flight.
   This robe of flesh I'll drop and rise
   to seize the everlasting prize
   And shout while passing through the air
   farewell, farewell, sweet hour of prayer.

TELL IT TO JESUS

Traditional

1. Are you wear - y, are you heav - y - heart - ed?
2. Do the tears flow down your cheeks un - bid - den?

3.,4. *(See additional lyrics)*

Tell it to Je - sus, Tell it to Je - sus; Are you griev - ing
Tell it ti Je - sus, Tell it to Je - sus; Have you sins that

o - ver joys de - part - ed? Tell it to Je - sus a - lone.
to men's eyes are hid - den? Tell it to Je - sus a - lone.

Additional Lyrics

3. Do you fear the gath'ring clouds of sorrow?
   Tell it to Jesus, Tell it to Jesus;
   Are you anxious what shall be tomorrow?
   Tell it to Jesus alone.
   REFRAIN

4. Are you troubled at the thought of dying?
   Tell it to Jesus, Tell it to Jesus;
   For Christ's coming kingdom are you sighing?
   Tell it to Jesus alone.
   REFRAIN

THERE IS A FOUNTAIN

Traditional

Additional Lyrics

2. The dying thief rejoiced to see
   That fountain in his day;
   And there may I, though vile as he,
   Wash all my sins away:...

3. Dear dying Lamb, Thy precious blood
   Shall never lose its power,
   Till all the ransomed Church of God
   Be saved, to sin no more:...

4. E'er since by faith, I saw the stream
   Thy flowing wounds supply,
   Redeeming love has been my theme,
   And shall be till I die:...

4. Then in a nobler, sweeter song,
   I'll sing Thy power to save,
   When this poor lisping, stamm'ring tongue
   Lies silent in the grave:... Amen.

WAYFARING STRANGER

Traditional American Folksong

I am a

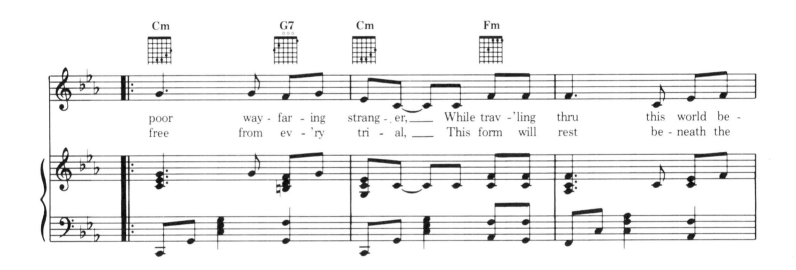

poor   way-far-ing   strang-er,___   While trav-'ling   thru   this world be-
free   from ev-'ry   tri-al, ___   This form will   rest   be-neath the

low;   There is   no   sick-   ness, toil,   nor   dan-ger.___   In that   bright
sod;   I'll   drop the   cross   of   self-de-   ni-al,___   And   en-ter

WE'LL UNDERSTAND IT BETTER
BY AND BY

Traditional

Moderately slow

1. We are of-ten tossed and driv-en on the
2.-4. (See additional lyrics)

rest-less sea of time, Som-ber skies and howl-ing tem-pests oft suc-ceed a bright sun-shine, In that

land of per-fect day, when the mists have rolled a-way, We will un-der-stand it bet-ter by and

Additional Lyrics

2. We are often destitute of the things that life demands,
   Want of food and want of shelter, thirsty hills and barren lands,
   We are trusting in the Lord, and according to His word,
   We will understand it better by and by.
   REFRAIN

3. Trials dark on every hand, and we cannot understand,
   All the ways that God would lead us to that blessed Promised Land;
   But He guides us with His eye and we'll follow till we die,
   For we'll understand it better by and by.
   REFRAIN

4. Temptations, hidden snares often take us unawares,
   And our hearts are made to bleed for a thoughtless word or deed,
   And we wonder why the test when we try to do our best,
   But we'll understand it better by and by.
   REFRAIN

WE'RE MARCHING TO ZION

Traditional

Additional Lyrics

2. Let those refuse to sing
   Who never knew our God;
   But children of the heav'nly King,
   But children of the heav'nly King,
   May speak their joys abroad,
   May speak their joys abroad.
   REFRAIN

3. The hill of Zion yields
   A thousand sacred sweets,
   Before we reach the heav'nly fields,
   Before we reach the heav'nly fields,
   Or walk the golden streets,
   Or walk the golden streets.
   REFRAIN

4. Then let our songs abound,
   And ev'ry tear be dry;
   We're marching thru Immanuel's ground,
   We're marching thru Immanuel's ground,
   To fairer worlds on high,
   To fairer worlds on high.
   REFRAIN

WHAT A FRIEND WE HAVE IN JESUS

Words by JOSEPH SCRIVEN
Music by CHARLES C. CONVERSE

Moderately

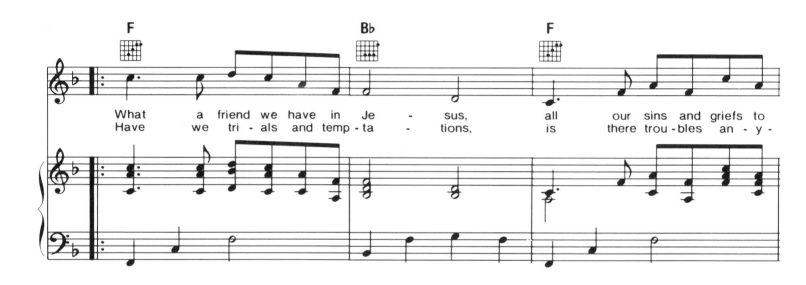

What a friend we have in Je - sus, all our sins and griefs to
Have we tri - als and temp - ta - tions, is there trou - bles an - y -

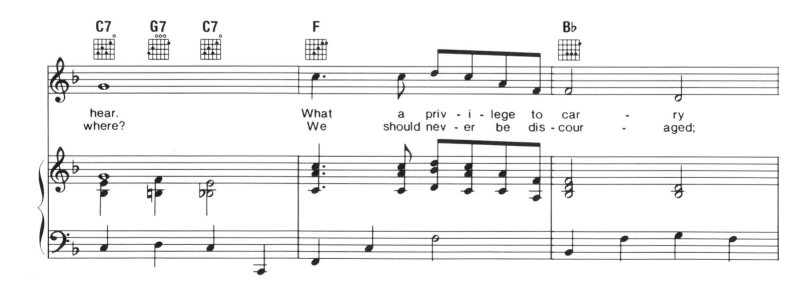

hear.
where?
What a priv - i - lege to car - ry
We should nev - er be dis - cour - aged;

3. Are we weak and heavy laden,
   cumbered with a load of care?
   Precious Savior still our refuge;
   take it to the Lord in prayer.
   Do thy friends despise, forsake thee?
   Take it to the Lord in prayer.
   In His arms He'll take and shield thee;
   thou will find a solace there.

WHEN WE ALL GET TO HEAVEN

Traditional

Additional Lyrics

2. While we walk the pilgrim pathway,
Clouds will overspread the sky;
But when trav'ling days are over,
Not a shadow, not a sigh!
REFRAIN

3. Let us then be true and faithful,
Trusting, serving ev'ryday.
Just one glimpse of Him in glory
Will the toils of life repay.
REFRAIN

4. Onward to the prize before us!
Soon His beauty we'll behold.
Soon the pearly gates will open;
We shall tread the streets of gold.
REFRAIN

WHITER THAN SNOW

Traditional

1. Lord Je - sus, I long to be per - fect - ly whole; I
2.-4. *(See additional lyrics)*

want Thee for - ev - er to live in my soul, Break

down ev - ery i - dol, cast out ev - ery foe; Now

Additional Lyrics

2. Lord Jesus, look down from Thy throne in the skies,
   And help me to make a complete sacrifice;
   I give up myself, and whatever I know,
   Now wash me and I shall be whiter than snow.
   REFRAIN

3. Lord Jesus, for this I most humbly entreat,
   I wait, blessed Lord, at Thy crucified feet;
   By faith, for my cleansing I see Thy blood flow,
   Now wash me and I shall be whiter than snow.
   REFRAIN

4. Lord Jesus, Thou seeest I patiently wait,
   Come now, and within me a new heart create;
   To those who have sought Thee, Thou never saidst "No,"
   Now wash me and I shall be whiter than snow.
   REFRAIN

WHEN THE ROLL IS CALLED UP YONDER

Traditional

When the trum-pet of the Lord shall sound, and
bright and cloud-less morn-ing when the

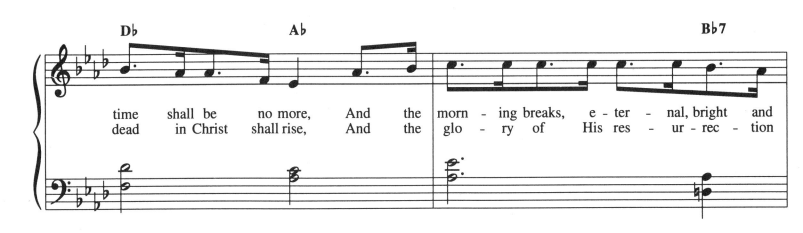

time shall be no more, And the morn-ing breaks, e-ter-nal, bright and
dead in Christ shall rise, And the glo-ry of His res-ur-rec-tion

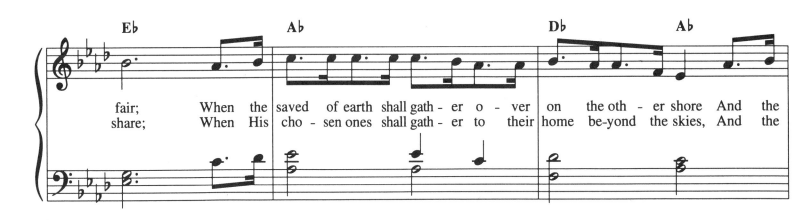

fair; When the saved of earth shall gath-er o-ver on the oth-er shore And the
share; When His cho-sen ones shall gath-er to their home be-yond the skies, And the

talk of all His won-drous love and care; Then when all of life is o-ver and our

work on earth is done And the roll is called up yon-der, I'll be there! When the

roll _____ is called up yon - der, When the roll _____ is called up yon - der, When the

roll _____ is called up yon - der, When the roll is called up yon-der, I'll be there!